365 INSPIR

self

&

spirit

*

365 INSPIRATIONS

self

&

spirit

DUNCAN BAIRD PUBLISHERS

LONDON

365 Inspirations: Self & Spirit

General Editor: Emma Maule

First published in 2007 by
Duncan Baird Publishers Ltd
Sixth Floor, Castle House
75–76 Wells Street, London W1T 3QH

Conceived, created and designed by Duncan Baird Publishers

Assistant Editor: Kirty Topiwala
Managing Designer: Clare Thorpe
Designer: Louise Leffler
Picture research: Susannah Stone

British Library Cataloguing-in-Publication Data:
A catalogue record for this book is available from the British Library
10 9 8 7 6 5 4 3 2 1
ISBN: 978-1-84483-471-6

Typeset in Gill Sans and New Berolina
Colour reproduction by Scanhouse, Malaysia
Printed by Imago, Thailand

NOTES
Abbreviations used throughout this book:
CE Common Era (the equivalent of AD)
BCE Before the Common Era (the equivalent of BC)
b. born, d. died

Contents

Foreword

Self-esteem, we're told, is one of the necessary facets in the kaleidoscope of the whole self. Without it we starve in life's shadows instead of being nourished by the sunlight of our true destiny. But why should we value ourselves so much? The answer comes in a flash: because self and spirit are one and the same.

There's a paradox here, and an enriching one. Spirit is the ineffable, priceless thing inside us all, and the link that connects all human beings in a profound kinship, transcending differences of age, race, class and gender. It is, according to many sages, divinity itself – which connects with the view that all that is precious in our lives is to be found within.

Yet at the same time the spirit is what makes us, uniquely, who we are. It is indivisible, inexpressibly profound and forever mysterious.

The new spirituality has no canonical scripture but many prized texts, from the Tao Te Ching to the mystic poems of Rumi. All inspiring insights, even those of pragmatic Romans like Marcus Aurelius, are esteemed. This book presents a collection of illuminating wisdom on self and spirit. Let the light refracted in 365 lovely prisms flower in your heart.

The inner self

Self-awareness

1 Inward, outward

The outward freedom that we shall attain will
only be in exact proportion to the inward freedom
to which we may have grown at a given moment.
And if this is a correct view of freedom, our chief
energy must be concentrated on achieving reform
from within.

Mahatma Gandhi (1869–1948), India

2 Revealing annoyances

Everything that irritates us about
others can lead us to an understanding
of ourselves.

Carl Jung (1875–1961), Switzerland

3 Different selves

Whenever two people meet there are
really six people present.
There is each man as he sees himself, each
man as the other person sees him, and
each man as he really is.

William James (1842–1910), USA

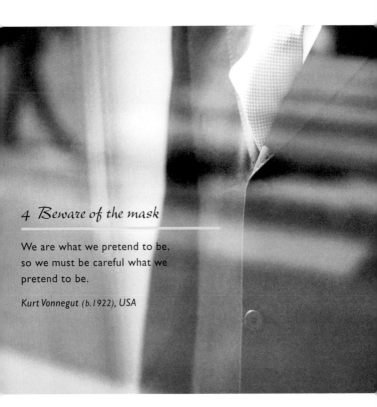

4 Beware of the mask

We are what we pretend to be,
so we must be careful what we
pretend to be.

Kurt Vonnegut (b.1922), USA

5 All too familiar

The aspects of things that are
most important to us are hidden
because of their simplicity
and familiarity.

Ludwig Wittgenstein (1889–1951),
Austria/England

6 *Self light*

Self light
glows through
your dark skin,
feels warm
on your skin,
as if you are
sitting by the
palace hearth.

Self light
knows nothing
of dark cells,
organs, only
guessed at,
like life in distant
colonies the king
has never visited.

Gabriella Venditti (b.1976), Italy

Self-esteem

7 Personal worth

A person's worth in this world is estimated according to the value they put on themselves.

Jean de La Bruyère (1645–1696), France

8 Signpost of destiny

What a man thinks of himself, that it is which determines, or rather indicates, his fate.

Henry David Thoreau (1817–1862), USA

9 Wellness clinic

Of all our infirmities, the most
savage is to despise our being.

Michel de Montaigne (1533–1592), France

10 Full circle

Argue for your limitations,
and sure enough, they're yours!

Richard Bach (b.1936), USA

11 Equal desserts

You yourself, as much as anybody in the entire universe, deserve your love and affection.

The Buddha (c.563–c.483BCE), *India*

12 *Secret of life*

Trust yourself,
then you will know how to live.

Johann Wolfgang von Goethe (1749–1832), Germany

13 True wealth

A man's true state of power and riches is to be in himself.

Henry Ward Beecher (1813–1887), USA

14 The troubled peacock

People are crying up the rich
and variegated plumage of the
peacock, and he is himself blushing
at the sight of his ugly feet.

Shaikh Sa'di Shirazi (1194–1292), Persia

15 Snail and star

My calling is as great as snail or star,
    neither more nor less.

From my shell my glory blazes,
    bright and far,
and my love-light slithers humbly
    through God's grass.

Andrea de Torres (b.1950), Guatemala

Emotions

16 Blind alley

Emotion turning back on itself,
and not leading on to thought or action,
is the element of madness.

John Sterling (1806–1844), Scotland/England

17 Emotional alchemy

There can be no transforming of darkness
into light and of apathy into movement
without emotion.

Carl Jung (1875–1961), Switzerland

18 In service

Let's not forget that the little emotions are the
great captains of our lives and we obey them
without realizing it.

Vincent van Gogh (1853–1890), Netherlands/France

19 Battle of the wolves

A Native American grandfather was talking to his
grandson about how he felt.

He said,

> "I feel as if I have two wolves fighting in my heart.
> One wolf is the vengeful, angry, violent one.
> The other wolf is the loving, compassionate one."

The grandson asked him,

> "Which wolf will win the fight in your heart?"

The grandfather answered,

> "The one I feed."

Native American parable

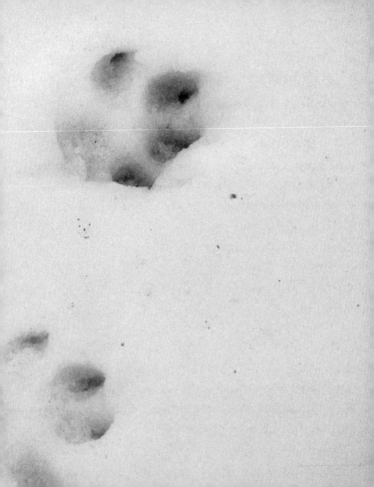

20 Unintended

Any emotion, if it is sincere,
is involuntary.

Mark Twain (1835–1910), USA

21 *Brain and soul*

There can be no knowledge without emotion. We may be aware of a truth, yet until we have felt its force, it is not ours. To the cognition of the brain must be added the experience of the soul.

Arnold Bennett (1867–1931), England/France

22 Release yourself

One's suffering disappears when one lets oneself go, when one yields – even to sadness.

Antoine de Saint-Exupéry (1900–1944), France

The senses

23 Against reason

"Reason" is the cause of our falsification
        of the evidence of the senses.
In so far as the senses show becoming,
        passing away, change, they do not lie.

Friedrich Nietzsche (1844–1900), Germany

24 Each part and tag

Through me forbidden voices,
Voices of sexes and lusts,
    voices veil'd and I remove the veil ...
I believe in the flesh and the appetites,
Seeing, hearing and feeling are miracles,
    and each part and tag of me is
    a miracle.

Walt Whitman (1819–1892), USA

25 Roadblock

The strong man is the one who is able
to intercept at will the communication
between the senses and the mind.

Napoleon Bonaparte (1769–1821), Italy/France

26 Too much information

I was afraid that by observing objects with
my eyes and trying to comprehend them
with each of my other senses I might blind
my soul altogether.

Socrates (469–399 BCE), Greece

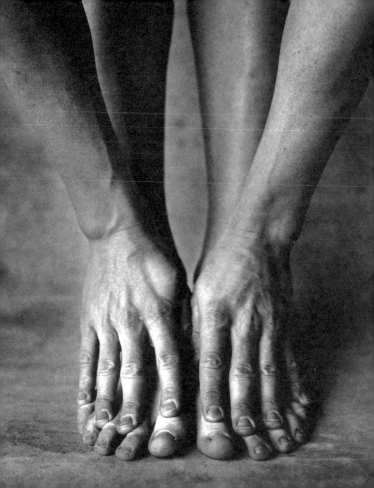

27 Act and feel

To live is not merely to breathe: it is to act; it is to make use of our organs, senses, faculties – of all those parts of ourselves which give us the feeling of existence.

Jean-Jacques Rousseau (1712–1778), Switzerland/France

28 Use these gifts

I do not feel obliged to believe that the same God who has endowed us with sense, reason and intellect has intended us to forgo their use.

Galileo Galilei (1564–1642), Italy

29 Sympathetic strings

We are all instruments endowed with
feeling and memory. Our senses are
so many strings that are struck by
surrounding objects and that also
frequently strike themselves.

Denis Diderot (1713–1784), France

30 Imperfections

Half of us are blind,
few of us feel,
and we are all deaf.

William Osler (1849–1919), Canada

Meditation

31 Speaking through silence

Meditation is the tongue of the soul
and the language of our spirit.

Jeremy Taylor (1613–1667), England

32 Smooth running

In deep meditation the flow of
concentration is continuous like
the flow of oil.

Patanjali (2nd century BCE),
from the Yoga Sutra, India

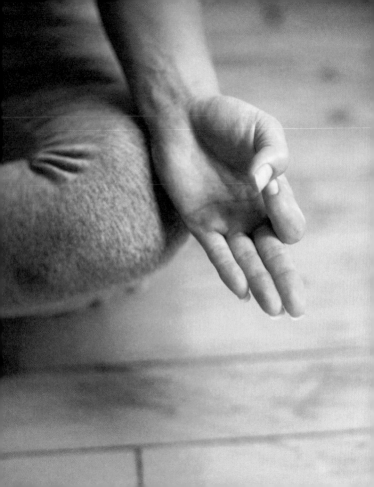

33 Directional thinking

As the fletcher whittles and makes straight his arrows, so the master directs his straying thoughts.

The Buddha (c.563–c.483 BCE), in the Dhammapada, *India*

34 All one

An ancient master said,
"The mountains, the rivers, the whole earth,
the entire array of phenomena are all oneself."
If you can absorb the essence of this message,
there are no activities outside of meditation:

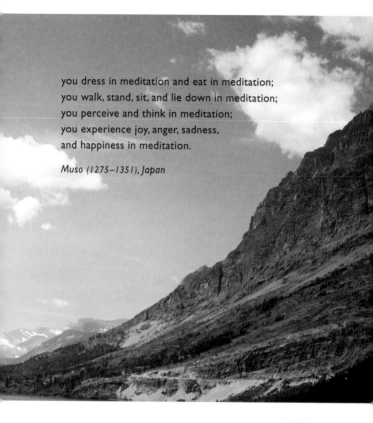

you dress in meditation and eat in meditation;
you walk, stand, sit, and lie down in meditation;
you perceive and think in meditation;
you experience joy, anger, sadness,
and happiness in meditation.

Muso (1275–1351), Japan

35 Signs of progress

Health,
a light body,
freedom from cravings,
a glowing skin,
sonorous voice,
fragrance of body:
these signs indicate progress in the
    practice of meditation.

From the Shvetashvatara Upanishad

36 Merging with the infinite

Meditation is the dissolution of
thoughts in Eternal awareness or Pure
consciousness without objectification,
knowing without thinking, merging
finitude in infinity.

Swami Sivananda (1887–1963), India/Malaysia

37 Clear seeing

Seek truth in meditation,
not in mouldy books.
Look in the sky to find the moon,
not in the pond.

Persian proverb

38 A quiet flame

When meditation is mastered,
the mind is unwavering
like the flame of a lamp
in a windless place.

From the Bhagavad Gita
(1st–2nd century BCE), India

39 No time to waste

The affairs of the world will go on forever.
Do not delay the practice of meditation.

Jetsun Milarepa (c.1052–c.1135), Tibet

40 Jacob's ladder

Happy the heart that keeps its twilight hour,
And, in the depths of heavenly peace reclined,
Loves to commune with thoughts of tender power,
Thoughts that ascend, like angels beautiful,
A shining Jacob's ladder of the mind!

Paul Hamilton Hayne (1830–1886), USA

Peace

41 Pure vastness

The mind should be a vastness like the sky. Mental events should be allowed to disperse like clouds.

Longchenpa (1308–1363), Tibet

42 Golden slipper

If we have not quiet in our minds,
outward comfort will do no more
for us than a golden slipper on
a gouty foot.

John Bunyan (1628–1688), England

43 Tick tock

Quiet minds can't be perplexed
or frightened, but go on in fortune
or misfortune at their own private pace,
like a clock during a thunderstorm.

Robert Louis Stevenson (1850–1894), Scotland

44 A winged moment

Didst thou ever descry a glorious
eternity in a winged moment of time?
Didst thou ever see a bright infinite
in the narrow point of an object?
Then thou knowest what spirit means –
the spire top whither all things ascend
harmoniously and where they meet
and sit contented in an unfathomed
depth of life.

Peter Sterry (1613–1672), England

45 Recipe for happiness

Do you want long life and happiness? ...
Strive for peace with all your heart.

Psalms 34:12,14

46 Lens of peace

You cannot perceive beauty but with a serene mind.

Henry David Thoreau (1817–1862), USA

47 Inspired awareness

When you are inspired by some great purpose,
    all your thoughts break their bonds.
Your mind transcends limitations, your consciousness
    expands in every direction and you find yourself
    in a new, great and wonderful world.
Dormant forces, faculties and talents become alive,
    and you discover yourself to be a greater person
    by far than you ever dreamed yourself to be.

Patanjali (2nd century BCE), from the Yoga Sutra, *India*

48 The mind's way

Peace cannot be achieved through violence, it can only be attained through understanding.

Ralph Waldo Emerson
(1803–1882), USA

49 Bliss of the heart

Not that light is holy,
     but that the holy is the light –
Only by seeing, by being,
     we know,
Rapt, breath stilled,
     bliss of the heart.

Kathleen Raine (1908–2003), England

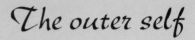

The outer self

50 *Healthy and happy*

Health is the vital principle of bliss, and exercise, of health.

James Thomson (1700–1748), Scotland/Ireland

51 First liberty

In health there is freedom.
Health is the first of all liberties.

Henri-Frédéric Amiel (1828–1881), Switzerland

52 Fine tuning

The body is like a piano, and happiness is like music.
It is needful to have the instrument in good order.

Henry Ward Beecher (1813–1887), USA

53 Scary

He who sings frightens away his ills.

Miguel de Cervantes (1547–1616), Spain

54 Better than gold

Better off poor, healthy and fit than rich and afflicted in body.
Health and fitness are better than any gold, and a robust
body than countless riches.

Ecclesiasticus 30:14–15

55 Second blessing

Look to your health; and if you have it, praise God,
and value it next to a good conscience;
for health is the second blessing that we
mortals are capable of;
a blessing that money cannot buy.

Izaak Walton (1593–1683), England

56 Health's bloom

Cheerfulness is the very flower of health.

Japanese proverb

57 Fit for our purpose

To preserve health is a moral and religious duty, for health is the basis of all social virtues. We can no longer be useful when we are not well.

Samuel Johnson (1709–1784), England

58 Mind and body

The mind has great influence over the body, and maladies often have their origin there.

Molière (1622–1673), France

59 Harmony

The part can never be well
unless the whole is well.

Plato (c.429–c.347 BCE), Greece

Body

60 *Automaton*

Bodily decay is gloomy in prospect,
but of all human contemplations the most
abhorrent is body without mind.

Thomas Jefferson (1762–1826), USA

61 *Sooner or later*

Those who think they have no time for bodily
exercise will sooner or later have to find time
for illness.

Edward Stanley (1799–1869), England

62 Pointing the finger

Be sure that it is not you that is mortal, but only your body.
For that man whom your outward form reveals is not yourself;
the spirit is the true self, not that physical figure which can be
pointed out by your finger.

Cicero (c.106–43 BCE), Rome

63 Green fingers

Our bodies are our gardens;
to the which our wills are gardeners.

William Shakespeare (1564–1616),
from Othello, *England*

64 Windows

The body is a house of many
windows: there we all sit, showing
ourselves and crying on the
passers-by to come and love us.

Robert Louis Stevenson (1850–1894), Scotland

65 *Secrets* and *marvels*

The body is a marvellous machine ...
a chemical laboratory, a power-house.
Every movement, voluntary or
involuntary, full of secrets and marvels!

Theodor Herzl (1860–1904), Austria

66 Sacred frame

There is but one temple in the universe and that is the body of man.

Novalis (1772–1801), Germany

67 Silent company

I live in company with a body,
a silent companion, exacting
and eternal.

Eugène Delacroix (1798–1863), France

Self-expression

68 The triple self

I hold a beast,
an angel and a madman in me,
and my enquiry is as to their working,
and my problem is their subjugation and victory,
downthrow and upheaval,
and my effort is their self-expression.

Dylan Thomas (1914–1953), Wales

69 The art of character

One thing is needful – to "give style" to one's character –
   a great and rare art!
It is practised by those who survey all the strengths and
   weaknesses of their nature and then fit them into
   an artistic plan until every one of them appears as
   art and reason and even weaknesses delight the eye.

Friedrich Nietzsche (1844–1900), Germany

70 Words like stones

Like stones, words are laborious and unforgiving, and the fitting of them together, like the fitting of stones, demands great patience and strength of purpose and particular skill.

Edmund Morrison (b.1940), England

71 Well equipped

Nature gave us one tongue and two ears so we could hear twice as much as we speak.

Epictetus (c.55–c.135), Greece

72 Never apologize

Never apologize for showing feeling. When you do so, you apologize for truth.

Benjamin Disraeli (1804–1881), England

73 A paradox

Music expresses that which
cannot be put into words and
that which cannot remain silent.

Victor Hugo (1802–1885), France

74 Art, music, poetry

Life has been your art.
You have set yourself to music.
Your days are your sonnets.

Oscar Wilde (1854–1900), England

75 Your own gift

Insist on yourself; never imitate.
Your own gift you can present every moment
with the cumulative force of a whole life's
cultivation; but of the adopted talent of another
you have only an extemporaneous half-possession.

Ralph Waldo Emerson (1803–1882), USA

76 Extravagance

I fear chiefly lest my expression may not be extravagant enough, may not wander far enough beyond the narrow limit of my daily experience, so as to be adequate to the truth of which I have been convinced.

Extravagance! It depends on how you are yarded.

Henry David Thoreau (1817–1862), USA

Self and cosmos

77 Hidden harmony

In all chaos there is a Cosmos,
in all disorder a secret order.

Carl Jung (1875–1961), Switzerland

78 In training

Life is the soul's nursery —
its training place for the destinies
of eternity.

William Makepeace Thackeray (1811–1863), England

79 Calm and bright

I saw Eternity the other night
Like a great *Ring* of pure endless light,
All calm, as it was bright;
And round beneath it,
Time in hours, days, years
Driven by the spheres
Like a vast shadow moved.

Henry Vaughan (1621–1695), Wales

80 Lit from within

Throughout my whole life, during every
minute of it, the world has been gradually
lighting up and blazing before my eyes
until it has come to surround me,
entirely lit up from within.

Pierre Teilhard de Chardin (1881–1955), France

81 Cosmic intelligence

Deem you that only you have thought and sense,
While heaven and all its wonders, sun and earth,
Scorned in your dullness, lack intelligence?
Fool! What produced you? These things gave you birth:
So have they mind and God.

Tommaso Campanella (1568–1639), Italy

82 Absolute perfection

God who is eternally complete,
who directs the stars,
who is the master of fates,
who elevates man from his lowliness to Himself,
who speaks from the cosmos to every single human soul,
is the most brilliant manifestation of the goal of perfection to date.

Alfred Adler (1870–1937), Austria

83 Totality

He who has seen present things has seen all,
both everything which has taken place from all eternity
      and everything which will be for time without end;
for all things are of one kin and of one form.

Marcus Aurelius (121–180), Rome

84 Ocean of truth

I do not know what I may appear to the world, but to myself I seem to have been only like a boy playing on the seashore, diverting myself in now and then finding a smoother pebble or a prettier shell than ordinary, whilst the great ocean of truth lay all undiscovered before me.

Sir Isaac Newton (1642–1727), England

85 Atomic query

Why I came here, I know not;
where I shall go it is useless to inquire –
in the midst of myriads of the living and
the dead worlds, stars, systems, infinity,
why should I be anxious about an atom?

Lord Byron (1788–1824), England

Pleasure

86 Gain and loss

The greatest and noblest pleasure which men can have in this world
is to discover new truths; and the next is to shake off old prejudices.

Frederick the Great (1712–1786), Prussia

87 Arrivals and departures

In life there is nothing more unexpected and surprising than the
        arrivals and departures of pleasure.
If we find it in one place today, it is vain to seek it there tomorrow.
You cannot lay a trap for it.

Alexander Smith (1830–1867), Scotland

88 Modest enjoyment

Tranquil pleasures last the longest; we are not fitted to bear the burden of great joys.

Christian Nestell Bovee (1820–1904), USA

89 Pleasant prospects

Joy is never in our power and pleasure often is.

C.S. Lewis (1898–1963), Ireland/England

90 *Cautious approach*

Do not bite at the bait of pleasure,
till you know there is no hook
beneath it.

Thomas Jefferson (1762–1826), USA

91 Satisfaction

The noblest pleasure is the joy of understanding.

Leonardo da Vinci (1452–1519), Italy

92 Overshooting

Most men pursue pleasure with such breathless haste that they hurry past it.

Søren Kierkegaard (1813–1855), Denmark

93 The sublime fountain

You are quaffing drink from a hundred fountains:
whenever any of these hundred yields less, your
pleasure is diminished. But when the sublime
fountain gushes from within you, no longer need
you steal from the other fountains.

Jalil al-Din Rumi (1207–1273), Persia

94 Talking cure

For let me tell you, that the more
the pleasures of the body fade away,
the greater to me is the pleasure
and charm of conversation.

Plato (c.429–c.347 BCE), Greece

95 Mature wisdom

Old age has been charged with being insensible to pleasure
and to enjoyments arising from the gratification of the senses,
a most blessed and heavenly effect, truly, if it eases us of what
in youth was the sorest plague of life.

Cicero (c.106–43 BCE), Rome

96 True perspective

The important question is not, what will yield
to man a few scattered pleasures, but what will
render his life happy on the whole amount.

Joseph Addison (1672–1719), England

Celebration

97 Battle song

Life has meaning only in the struggle. Triumph or defeat is in the hands of the Gods. So let us celebrate the struggle!

Swahili warrior song

98 Hallelujah

Rejoice in the Lord always; again I will say, Rejoice.

Philippians 4:4

99 Open day

The windows of my soul I throw
Wide open to the sun.

John Greenleaf Whittier (1807–1892), USA

100 I celebrate myself

I celebrate myself and sing myself;
And what I assume you shall assume;
For every atom belonging to me, as good belongs to you.
I loaf and invite my Soul;
I lean and loaf at my ease,
        observing a spear of summer grass.
Houses and rooms are full of perfumes –
        the shelves are crowded with perfumes;
I breathe the fragrance myself, and know it and like it;
The distillation would intoxicate me also,
        but I shall not let it.
The atmosphere is not a perfume –
        it has no taste of the distillation – it is odorless;
It is for my mouth forever – I am in love with it;
I will go to the bank by the wood,
        and become undisguised and naked;
I am mad for it to be in contact with me.

Walt Whitman (1819–1892), from "Song of Myself", USA

101 Hiawatha's greeting

Then the joyous Hiawatha
Cried aloud and spake in this wise:
"Beautiful is the sun, O strangers,
When you come so far to see us!
All our town in peace awaits you,
All our doors stand open for you;
You shall enter all our wigwams,
For the heart's right hand we give you.

"Never bloomed the earth so gayly,
Never shone the sun so brightly,
As today they shine and blossom
When you come so far to see us!
Never was our lake so tranquil,
Nor so free from rocks, and sand-bars;
For your birch canoe in passing
Has removed both rock and sand-bar.

"Never before had our tobacco
Such a sweet and pleasant flavor,
Never the broad leaves of our cornfields
Were so beautiful to look on,
As they seem to us this morning,
When you come so far to see us!"

Henry Wadsworth Longfellow (1807–1882), USA

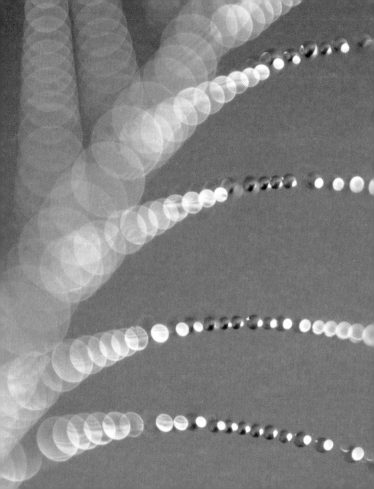

Values and qualities

Creativity

Commitment

Courage

Self-control

Originality

Love

Compassion

Integrity

Patience

Goodness

Wisdom

102 Breaking free

Be daring, be different, be impractical, be anything that will assert integrity of purpose and imaginative vision against the play-it-safers, the creatures of the commonplace, the slaves of the ordinary.

Sir Cecil Beaton (1904–1980), England

103 Playtime

The creation of something new is not accomplished by the intellect but by the play instinct acting from inner necessity. The creative mind plays with the objects it loves.

Carl Jung (1875–1961), Switzerland

104 Master builder

If you have built castles in the air,
your work need not be lost;
that is where they should be.
Now put the foundations
        under them.

Henry David Thoreau (1817–1862), USA

105 The right question

You see things:
you say "Why?"
But I dream things that never are:
and say "Why not?"

*George Bernard Shaw (1856–1950),
Ireland/England*

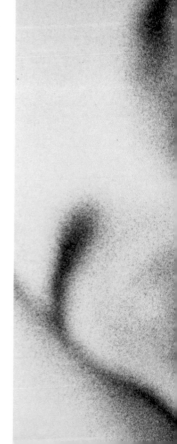

106 *Step by step*

No great thing is created suddenly.

Epictetus (c.55–c.135), Greece

107 Mixed metaphor

The faculty of imagination is both the rudder and the bridle of the senses.

Leonardo da Vinci (1452–1519), Italy

108 *Just imagine*

Imagination is the living power and prime agent of all human perception.

Samuel Taylor Coleridge (1772–1834), England

Commitment

109 Hard choices

Compromise is but the sacrifice of one right or good in the hope of retaining another – too often ending in the loss of both.

Tryon Edwards (1809–1894), USA

110 True to his word

He who is most slow in making a promise is the most faithful in performance of it.

Jean-Jacques Rousseau (1712–1778), Switzerland/France

111 *No half measures*

Wheresoever you go,
go with all your heart.

Confucius (551–479 BCE), China

112 *Action point*

Vision is not enough.
It must be combined with venture.
It is not enough to stare up the steps,
we must step up the stairs.

Václav Havel (b.1936), Czechoslovakia

113 Invincible

The most powerful weapon on earth is the human soul on fire.

Ferdinand Foch (1851–1929), France

114 Aim high

Make no little plans; they have no magic to stir men's blood and probably will themselves not be realized. Make big plans; aim high in hope and work, remembering that a noble, logical diagram once recorded will not die.

Daniel H. Burnham (1846–1912), USA

Courage

115 A curiosity

It is curious that physical courage should be so common in the world and moral courage so rare.

Mark Twain (1835–1910), USA

116 On audacity

To dare is to lose one's footing momentarily. To not dare is to lose oneself.

Søren Kierkegaard (1813–1855), Denmark

117 Home security

Courage is reckoned the greatest of all virtues;
because, unless a man has that virtue,
he has no security for preserving any other.

Samuel Johnson (1709–1784), England

118 Front line

Courage is not simply one of the virtues,
but the form of every virtue at the testing point.

C.S. Lewis (1898–1963), Ireland/England

119 Good listener

Courage is what it takes to stand up and speak;
courage is also what it takes to sit down and listen.

Sir Winston Churchill (1874–1965), England

120 *What it takes*

Whatever you do, you need courage.
Whatever course you decide upon,
    there is always someone to tell
    you that you are wrong.
There are always difficulties arising
    that tempt you to believe your
    critics are right.
To map out a course of action and follow
    it to an end requires some of the
    same courage that a soldier needs.
Peace has its victories, but it takes brave
    men and women to win them.

Ralph Waldo Emerson (1803–1882), USA

Self-control

121 Sovereign of the self

I am, indeed, a king,
because I know how to rule myself.

Pietro Aretino (1492–1556), Italy

122 How to rule events

Not being able to govern events,
I govern myself, and apply myself to them,
if they will not apply themselves to me.

Michel de Montaigne (1533–1592), France

123 Heart and head

One ought to hold on to one's heart;
for if one lets it go, one soon loses
control of the head too.

Friedrich Nietzsche (1844–1900), Germany

124 The art of resistance

There is no allurement or enticement,
actual or imaginary, which a well-
disciplined mind may not surmount.
The *wish* to resist more than half
accomplishes the object.

Charlotte Dacre (1782–1841), England

125 Running aground

Not to have control over
the senses is like sailing in a
rudderless ship, bound to break
to pieces on coming in contact
with the very first rock.

Mahatma Gandhi (1869–1948), India

Originality

126 Self-creation

It is the mind which creates the world
    around us,
and even though we stand side by side
    in the same meadow,
my eyes will never see what is beheld by yours,
my heart will never stir to the emotions
    with which yours is touched.

George Gissing (1857–1903), England/France

127 The non-conformist

Once conform, once do what others do because they do it, and a kind of lethargy steals over all the finer senses of the soul.

Michel de Montaigne (1533–1592), France

128 Audience participation

Men often applaud an imitation and hiss the real thing.

Aesop (c.620 – c.560 BCE), Greece

129 Think again

All truly wise thoughts have been
thought already thousands of times;
but to make them truly ours,
we must think them over again
honestly, till they take root in our
personal experience.

Johann Wolfgang von Goethe (1749–1832), Germany

130 Different drummer

If a man does not keep pace with
his companions,
perhaps it is because he hears
a different drummer.
Let him step to the music
which he hears,
however measured or far away.

Henry David Thoreau (1817–1862), USA

131 Sincerity

The merit of originality is not novelty;
it is sincerity.
The believing man is the original man;
whatsoever he believes,
he believes it for himself,
not for another.

*Thomas Carlyle (1795–1881),
Scotland/England*

132 Question everything

Do not believe in anything simply because you have heard it.

Do not believe in anything simply because it is spoken and
rumoured by many.

Do not believe in anything simply because it is found written
in your religious books.

Do not believe in anything merely on the authority of your
teachers and elders.

Do not believe in traditions because they have been handed
down for many generations.

But after observation and analysis, when you find that
anything agrees with reason and is conducive to the
good and benefit of one and all, then accept it
and live up to it.

The Buddha (c.563 – c.483 BCE), *India*

Love

133 Refulgence

Love is not consolation. It is light.

Friedrich Nietzsche (1844–1900), Germany

134 Immeasurable wealth

Who, being loved, is poor?

Oscar Wilde (1854–1900), Ireland/England

135 Love is the answer

Love is all we have, the only way that each can help the other.

Euripides (c.480–406 BCE), Greece

136 Precious patient

Love never dies a natural death.
It dies because we don't know how to
 replenish its source.
It dies of blindness and errors and betrayals.
It dies of illness and wounds;
 it dies of weariness, of witherings,
 of tarnishings.

Anaïs Nin (1903–1977), France

137 Artwork

Love is a canvas furnished by Nature and
embroidered by imagination.

Voltaire (1694–1778), France

138 Let them be

Let the lover be disgraceful, crazy,
    absent-minded.
Someone sober will worry about
    events going badly.
Let the lover be.

Jalil al-Din Rumi (1207–1273), Persia

139 A vision of heaven

Love brings ecstasy and relieves
    loneliness.
In the union of love I have seen
In a mystic miniature the
    prefiguring vision
Of the heavens that saints and
    poets have imagined.

Bertrand Russell (1872–1970),
England/USA

140 Free love

Love withers under constraints;
     its very essence is liberty.
It is compatible neither with obedience,
     jealousy, nor fear:
it is there most pure, perfect, and unlimited where its
     votaries live in confidence, equality and unreserve.

Percy Bysshe Shelley (1792–1822), England/Italy

141 Men and women

For there is one thing I can safely say: that those bound by love must obey each other if they are to keep company long.
Love will not be constrained by mastery; when mastery comes, the God of love at once beats his wings, and farewell – he is gone.
Love is a thing as free as any spirit; women naturally desire liberty, and not to be constrained like slaves; and so do men, if I shall tell the truth.

Geoffrey Chaucer (1342–1400), England

142 Gentle flood

Let your love be like the misty rains,
coming softly, but flooding the river.

Malagasy proverb

143 Loved and lost

I hold it true, whate'er befall;
I feel it, when I sorrow most;
'Tis better to have loved and lost
Than never to have loved at all.

Alfred, Lord Tennyson (1809–1892), England

Compassion

144 Essential business

Compassion is not religious business,
it is human business,
it is not luxury,
it is essential for our own peace and mental stability,
it is essential for human survival.

His Holiness the 14th Dalai Lama (b.1935), Tibet

145 Feeling first

I would rather feel compassion than know the meaning of it.

Thomas Aquinas (1225–1274), Italy/France

146 *A problem shared*

By compassion we make others' misery our own, and so, by relieving them, we relieve ourselves also.

Sir Thomas Browne (1605–1682), England

147 *Sight and sound*

Kindness is the language which the deaf can hear and the blind can see.

Mark Twain (1835–1910), USA

148 Sun, moon and sky

Compassion is the wish-fulfilling gem, the auspicious jar from which the splendour of good fortune comes; it is the finest medicine from which happiness derives, because the disease of living beings is cured. It is the sun of pristine cognitions, the moon soothing afflictions. It is like the sky, studded with the stars of spotless qualities, always bringing about prosperity and bliss.

Longchenpa (1308–1363), Tibet

149 Foundations

Compassion is the basis of morality.

Arthur Schopenhauer (1788–1860), Germany

150 Sweet remembrance

Forget injuries, never forget kindness.

Confucius (551–479 BCE), China

151 Billions

Wherever there is a human being,
there is an opportunity for a kindness.

Seneca (c.4 BCE–c.65 CE), Rome

152 *Creativity*

Kindness in words creates confidence.
Kindness in thinking creates profoundness.
Kindness in giving creates love.

Lao Tzu (c.604 – c.531 BCE), from the Tao Te Ching, *China*

153 Graces

The best portion
of a good man's life –
his little, nameless, unremembered
acts of kindness and love.

William Wordsworth (1770–1850), England

154 *Unconditional*

When we come into contact with the other
person, our thoughts and actions should express
our mind of compassion, even if that person says
and does things that are not easy to accept.
We practise in this way until we see clearly
that our love is not contingent upon the other
person being lovable.

Thich Nhat Hanh (b.1926), Vietnam/France

Integrity

155 Fast and true

In matters of principle, stand like a rock;
in matters of taste, swim with the current.

Thomas Jefferson (1743–1826), USA

156 Jeopardy within

Have no fear of robbers or murderers. They
are external dangers, petty dangers. We should
fear ourselves. Prejudices are the real robbers;
vices the real murderers. The great dangers are
within us. Why worry about what threatens our
heads or purses? Let us think instead of what
threatens our souls.

Victor Hugo (1802–1885), France

157 Life lesson

Character is higher than intellect.

Ralph Waldo Emerson (1803–1882), USA

158 Next best thing

If we cannot live so as to be happy,
let us at least live so as to deserve it.

Immanuel Hermann von Fichte (1797–1879), Germany

159 *Safest path*

Whoever walks in integrity walks securely, but whoever follows perverse ways will be found out.

Proverbs *10:9*

160 To thine own self

To thine own self be true,
and it must follow,
as the night the day,
thou canst not then be false to any man.

William Shakespeare (1564–1616),
from Hamlet, *England*

161 Throwaway

The reputation of a thousand years may be determined by the conduct of one hour.

Japanese proverb

162 Time management

It takes less time to do a thing right, than it does to explain why you did it wrong.

Henry Wadsworth Longfellow (1807–1882), USA

163 Virtue's economics

No man can purchase his virtue too dear,
for it is the only thing whose value must
ever increase with the price it has cost us.
Our integrity is never worth so much as
when we have parted with our all to keep it.

Ovid (43 BCE – 17 CE), Rome

164 Drop by drop

If you add a little to a little,
and then do it again, soon
that little shall be much.

Hesiod (c.700 BCE), Greece

165 Healing by degrees

How poor are they that have
not patience!
What wound did ever heal but
by degrees?

William Shakespeare (1564–1616), from Othello, *England*

166 *All will be revealed*

Everything comes gradually
and at its appointed hour.

Ovid (43BCE–17CE), Rome

167 *Snail's pace*

Adopt the pace of nature:
her secret is patience.

Ralph Waldo Emerson (1803–1882), USA

168 Waiting for God

The Lord is good unto them that wait
for him, to the soul that seeketh him.

Lamentations *3:25*

169 Silent forces

The two most powerful warriors are
patience and time.

Leo Tolstoy (1828–1910), Russia

Goodness

170 Pure and free

On life's journey
Faith is nourishment,
Virtuous deeds are a shelter,
Wisdom is the light by day and
Right mindfulness is the protection by night.
If a man lives a pure life, nothing can destroy him;
If he has conquered greed, nothing can limit his freedom.

The Buddha (c.563–c.483BCE), *India*

171 Indomitable spirit

It's really a wonder that I haven't dropped all my ideals,
because they seem so absurd and impossible to carry out.
Yet I keep them, because in spite of everything I still
believe that people are really good at heart.

Anne Frank (1929–1945), Holland

172 Safe passage

He who cannot forgive breaks
the bridge over which he himself
must pass.

George Herbert (1593–1633), England

173 Stowaway

Our humanity is a poor thing, except for the
divinity that stirs within us.

Francis Bacon (1561–1626), England

174 Our qualities

Love, hope, fear, faith – these make humanity;
these are its sign and note and character.

Robert Browning (1812–1889), England

175 Human nature

Man is the only animal that laughs and weeps;
for he is the only animal that is struck by the
difference between what things are and what
they might have been.

William Hazlitt (1778–1830), England

176 Cancellation

I can forgive, but I cannot forget, is only
another way of saying, I will not forgive.
Forgiveness ought to be like a cancelled
note – torn in two, and burned up, so that
it never can be shown against one.

Henry Ward Beecher (1813–1887), USA

177 Little by little

Let no man think lightly of evil:
"It will not touch me."
Drop by drop the pitcher is filled,
and little by little the fool is filled
    with evil.
Let not a man think lightly of good:
"It cannot be for me."
Drop by drop the pitcher is filled,
and little by little the wise man is filled
    with merit.

The Buddha (c.563–c.483 BCE),
in the Dhammapada, *India*

178 Elevated thoughts

Whenever anyone has offended
me, I try to raise my soul so high
that the offence cannot reach it.

René Descartes (1596–1650), France

179 Aspirations

Have a heart that never hardens,
a temper that never tires, a touch
that never hurts.

Charles Dickens (1812–1870), England

Wisdom

180 Seeing through appearances

Appearances to the mind are of four kinds.
>   Things either are what they appear to be;
>   or they neither are, nor appear to be;
>   or they are, and do not appear to be;
>   or they are not, and yet appear to be.
Rightly to aim in all these cases is the wise man's task.

Epictetus (c.55–c.135), Greece

181 Great minds

Do not allow yourselves to be deceived: great minds are sceptical.

Friedrich Nietzsche (1844–1900), Germany

182 Practical wisdom

There is no good in arguing with the inevitable.
The only argument available with an east wind is
to put on your overcoat.

James Russell Lowell (1819–1891), USA

183 Tranquil soul

For the wise man, in so far as he is regarded as such,
is scarcely at all disturbed in spirit, but being conscious
of himself, and of God, and of things, by a certain eternal
necessity, never ceases to be, but always possesses true
acquiescence of his spirit.

Baruch Spinoza (1632–1677), Netherlands

184 Seed time

When planning for a year, plant corn.
When planning for a decade, plant trees.
When planning for life, train and educate
    people.

Chinese proverb

185 Time after time

Life can only be understood backwards,
but it must be lived forwards.

Søren Kierkegaard (1813–1855), Denmark

186 In brief

Love truth, and pardon error.

Voltaire (1694–1778), France

187 A life well lived

In childhood be modest,
in youth temperate,
in adulthood just,
and in old age prudent.

Socrates (469–399 BCE), Greece

188 Equations

Wisdom is to the soul what health is to the body.

César Vichard de Saint-Réal (1639–1692), France

189 New start

Begin at once to live, and count each separate day as a separate life.

Seneca (c.4 BCE–c.65 CE), Rome

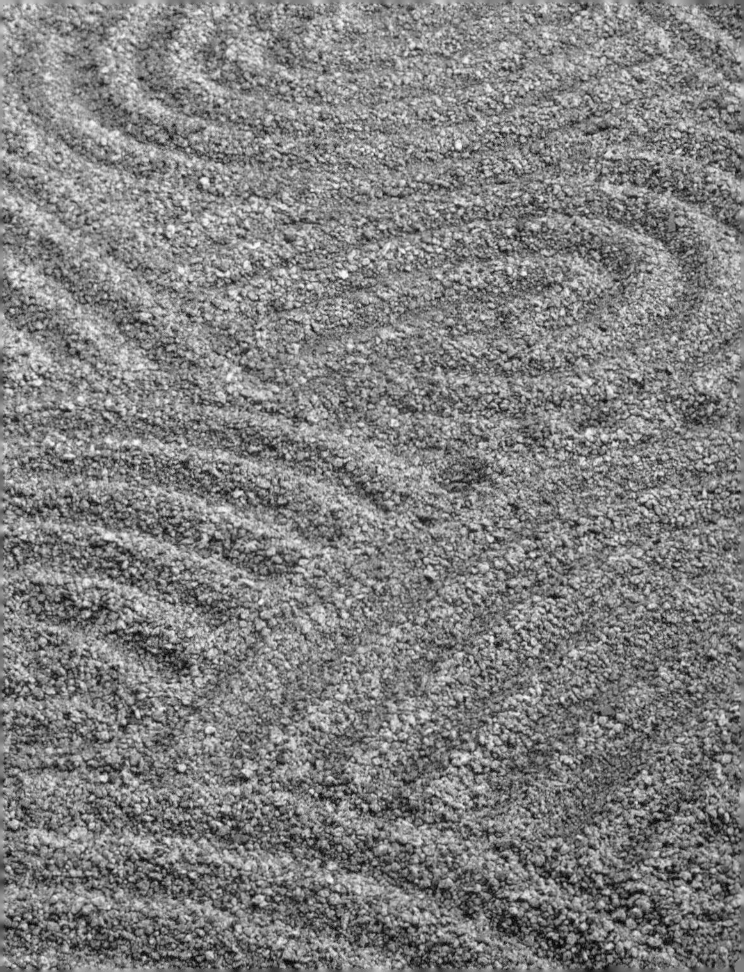

190 Eternal point

When there is no more separation between "this" and "that", it is called the still point of the Tao. At the still point in the centre of the circle one can see the infinite in all things.

Chuang Tzu (d.275 BCE), China

191 One requires another

Learning without thought is labour lost; and thought without learning is perilous.

Confucius (551–479 BCE), China

Family
and home

Childhood

192 Sensation's clock

Childhood is measured out by sounds and smells and sights, before the dark hour of reason grows.

John Betjeman (1906–1984), England

193 Young and old

Children find everything in nothing;
men find nothing in everything.

Giacomo Leopardi (1798–1837), Italy

194 Recipe

Bitter are the tears of a child:
    Sweeten them.
Deep are the thoughts of a child:
    Quiet them.
Sharp is the grief of a child:
    Take it from him.
Soft is the heart of a child:
    Do not harden it.

Pamela Glenconner (1871–1928), England

195 Busy little man

You are worried about seeing him spend
his early years in doing nothing. What!
Is it nothing to be happy? Nothing to skip,
play, and run around all day long? Never in
his life will he be so busy again.

Jean-Jacques Rousseau (1712–1778),
Switzerland/France

196 Privileged by innocence

Grown men can learn from very little children,
for the hearts of the little children are pure.
Therefore, the Great Spirit may show to them
many things which older people miss.

Oglala Sioux holy man

197 Soul's estate

All that was dear to us in our childhoods remains
in our hearts, a ghostly presence, a poignant
remembered flavour of heaven. These childhood
pastures are the places where our souls play still.

José Morazan (b.1952), Honduras

On these magic shores children at play are
for ever beaching their coracles. We too have
been there; we can still hear the sound of the
surf, though we shall land no more.

James M. Barrie (1860–1937), England

Ageing

199 Decades

Whoever, in middle age, attempts to realize the wishes
and hopes of his early youth, invariably deceives himself.
Each ten years of a man's life has its own fortunes, its own
hopes, its own desires.

Johann Wolfgang von Goethe (1749–1832), Germany

200 Well content

I am content in my later years. I have kept my good humour
and take neither myself nor the next person seriously.

Albert Einstein (1879–1955), Germany/USA

201 Evergreen

As I approve of a youth that has something of the old man in him, so I am no less pleased with an old man that has something of the youth. He that follows this rule may be old in body, but can never be so in mind.

Cicero (c.106–43 BCE), *Rome*

202 Forever young

It's not that age brings childhood back again,
Age merely shows what children we remain.

Johann Wolfgang von Goethe (1749–1832), Germany

203 Growth rates

We do not grow absolutely, chronologically.
We grow sometimes in one dimension, and not in
another; unevenly. We grow partially. We are relative.
We are mature in one realm, childish in another.
The past, present and future mingle and pull us
backward, forward, or fix us in the present.
We are made up of layers, cells, constellations.

Anaïs Nin (1903–1977), France

204 Star-filled sky

Age is opportunity no less
Than youth itself, though in another dress,
And as the evening twilight fades away
The sky is filled with stars, invisible by day.

Henry Wadsworth Longfellow (1807–1882), USA

205 New clothes

There has never been a time when you and I have not existed, nor will there be a time when we will cease to exist. As the same person inhabits the body through childhood, youth and old age, so too at the time of death he attains another body. The wise are not deluded by these changes.

From the Bhagavad Gita
(1st–2nd century BCE), India

206 Late blooms

It is always in season for old men to learn.

Aeschylus (525–456 BCE), Greece

207 *Life count*

So teach us to number our days,
that we may apply our hearts
unto wisdom.

Psalms 90:12

208 *At our heels*

Youth, large, lusty, loving – Youth,
    full of grace, force, fascination.
Do you know that Old Age may
      come after you with equal
     grace, force, fascination?

Walt Whitman (1819–1892), USA

Family

209 *Magnum opus*

The family is one of nature's masterpieces.

George Santayana (1863–1952), Spain/USA

210 *Blood ties*

In time of test, family is best.

Burmese proverb

211 Heaven's lieutenants

The voice of parents is the voice of gods,
for to their children they are heaven's
lieutenants.

William Shakespeare (1564–1616), England

212 Utopia

A happy family is but an earlier heaven.

John Bowring (1792–1872), England

213 Family ties

We cannot destroy kindred:
our chains stretch a little sometimes,
but they never break.

Madame de Sévigné (1626–1696), France

214 Culinary tips

Govern a family as you would cook a small fish – very gently.

Chinese proverb

215 Happy days

The happiest moments of my life have been the few which I have passed at home in the bosom of my family.

Thomas Jefferson (1743–1826), USA

216 Kinship rules

Family life is too intimate to be preserved by the spirit of justice. It can be sustained by a spirit of love which goes beyond justice.

Reinhold Niebuhr (1892–1971), USA

217 Parenting

Perhaps the greatest social service that can be rendered by anybody to this country and to mankind is to bring up a family.

Sir William Eden (1849–1915), England

Order

218 View from the tower

A well-ordered life is like climbing a tower; the view
halfway up is better than the view from the base,
and it steadily becomes finer as the horizon expands.

William Lyon Phelps (1865–1943), USA

219 Agree to differ

Not chaos-like together crush'd and bruis'd,
But, as the world, harmoniously confused:
Where order in variety we see,
And where tho' all things differ, all agree.

Alexander Pope (1688–1744), England

220 Threesome

Life nourishes.
Environment shapes.
Influences complete.

*Lao Tzu (c.604–c.531 BCE), from the
Tao Te Ching, China*

221 Underpinnings

Order is the sanity of the mind,
the health of the body, the peace
of the city, the security of the
State. As the beams to a house,
as the bones to the microcosm
of man, so is order to all things.

Robert Southey (1774–1843), England

222 *A contrast*

Be regular and orderly in your life,
so that you may be violent and
original in your work.

Gustave Flaubert (1821–1880), France

223 The moral dimension

He who has no taste for order,
will be often wrong in his judgment,
and seldom considerate or
conscientious in his actions.

Johann Kaspar Lavater (1741–1801), Switzerland

Home

224 Making a living

A man's homeland is wherever he prospers.

Aristophanes (c.448–385 BCE), Greece

225 Perfect world

In order for a person to attain the highest state
of being, he or she must first create a perfect
world in which to reach this highest state.

Choney Lama (1675–1748), Tibet

226 First things first

My precept to all who build is, that the owner should be
an ornament to the house, and not the house to the owner.

Cicero (c.106–43 BCE), Rome

227 Mystic circle

There is a magic in that little world, home;
it is a mystic circle that surrounds comforts and virtues
never known beyond its hallowed limits.

Robert Southey (1774–1843), England

228 Open sesame

Home is a name, a word, it is a strong one;
stronger than magician ever spoke, or spirit
ever answered to, in the strongest conjuration.

Charles Dickens (1812–1870), England

229 Householders

The strength of a nation derives from the
integrity of the home.

Confucius (551–479 BCE), China

230 Quiet haven

He is the happiest, be he king or peasant,
who finds peace in his home.

Johann Wolfgang von Goethe (1749–1832), Germany

Work

231 The weight of the world

Pray as though everything depended on God. Work as though everything depended on you.

St Augustine of Hippo (354–430), North Africa

232 Vocation

We work to become, not to acquire.

Elbert Hubbard (1856–1915), USA

233 Safe from ourselves

Work spares us from three evils: boredom, vice and need.

Voltaire (1694–1778), France

234 Nature at work

The finest workers in stone are not copper or steel tools, but the gentle touches of air and water working at their leisure with a liberal allowance of time.

Henry David Thoreau (1817–1862), USA

235 Job description

Work while you have the light. You are responsible for the talent that has been entrusted to you.

Henri Frédéric Amiel (1821–1881), Switzerland

236 Gladiator

It is not the critic who counts, not the man who points out how the strong man stumbled, or where the doer of deeds could have done better. The credit belongs to the man who is actually in the arena, whose face is marred by dust and sweat and blood, who strives valiantly, who errs and comes short again and again, who knows the great enthusiasms, the great devotions, and spends himself in a worthy cause, who at best knows achievement and who at the worst if he fails at least fails while daring greatly, so that his place shall never be with those cold and timid souls who know neither victory nor defeat.

Theodore Roosevelt (1858–1919), USA

237 One alternative

Work is a manifestation of love.
Anyone who finds his work distasteful should
abandon it altogether. Rather, take a begging bowl
out into the marketplace, in order to receive the
charity of those who work with happiness.

Eduardo Cuadra (1820–1903), Chile

238 System of balances

Good for the body is the work of the body,
good for the soul is the work of the soul,
and good for either is the work of the other.

Henry David Thoreau (1817–1862), USA

239 Brainwaves

A man is not idle because he is absorbed in thought.
There is a visible labour and there is an invisible labour.

Victor Hugo (1802–1885), France

240 Working dress

Opportunity is missed by most because it is dressed in
overalls and looks like work.

Thomas Edison (1847–1931), USA

Soul

Spirit

Mind

Thought

Happiness

Personal growth

Spirit

241 Lotus unfolding

The path of the spirit is not a line,
    but rather a flower.
Lines are time-bound, whereas the spirit's
    path is liberation from time:
    all-encompassing, never-ending.
Like a lotus of innumerable petals,
    our soul's journey is an
    unfolding of infinite self.

Sofia Khawati (1821–1890), Iran

242 Thumbnail sketch

Man: Half dust, half deity.

Lord Byron (1788–1824), England

243 Putting us straight

You don't have a soul. You are a Soul.
You have a body.

C.S. Lewis (1898–1963), Ireland/England

244 *Priorities*

Be careless in your dress if you must,
but keep a tidy soul.

Mark Twain (1835–1910), USA

245 Golden wings

Oh soul,
You worry too much.
You have seen your own strength.
You have seen your own beauty.
You have seen your golden wings.
About anything less,
Why do you worry?
You are in truth
The soul, of the soul, of the soul.

Jalil al-Din Rumi (1207–1273), Persia

246 *Soulful joy*

When you do things from your
soul you feel a river moving in
you, a joy. When action comes
from another part of you, the
feeling disappears.

Jalil al-Din Rumi (1207–1273), Persia

247 Morning prayer

Awake, my soul, and with the sun
The daily course of duty run.

Bishop Thomas Kenn (1637–1711), England

248 Two ways

There is one thing one has to have: either a soul that is
cheerful by nature, or a soul made cheerful by work, love,
art and knowledge.

Friedrich Nietzsche (1844–1900), Germany

249 Hidden beauty

The soul is placed in the body like a rough diamond,
and must be polished, or the lustre of it will never appear.

Daniel Defoe (1660–1731), England

250 Sweet nothings

What is mind? No matter. What is matter?
Never mind. What is the soul? It is immaterial.

Thomas Hood (1789–1845), England

251 Biblical wisdom

For what is a man profited, if he shall gain
the whole world, and lose his own soul?
Or what shall a man give in exchange for
his soul?

Matthew 16:26

252 Blood and dust

The soul, which is spirit, cannot dwell in dust;
it is carried along to dwell in the blood.

St Augustine of Hippo (354 – 430), North Africa

253 Life eternal

All of us have mortal bodies, composed of
perishable matter, but the soul lives forever:
it is a portion of the Deity housed in our bodies.

Flavius Josephus (c.37 – c.100 CE), Rome

Mind

254 Use your brain

It is not enough to have a good mind;
the main thing is to use it well.

René Descartes (1596–1650), France

255 Highest and lowest

The greatest minds, as they are capable
of the highest excellencies, are open
likewise to the greatest aberrations.

René Descartes (1596–1650), France

256 Dangerous powers

Only a brave person is willing to honestly admit,
and fearlessly to face, what a sincere and logical
mind discovers.

Rodan of Alexandria (1st century BCE), Egypt/Greece

257 Help yourself

The man who acquires the ability to take full possession of
his own mind may take possession of anything else to which
he is justly entitled.

Andrew Carnegie (1835–1919), Scotland/USA

258 The brain is wider ...

The Brain – is wider than the Sky –
For – put them side by side –
The one the other will contain
With ease – and You – beside –

The Brain is deeper than the sea –
For – hold them – Blue to Blue –
The one the other will absorb –
As Sponges – Buckets – do –

The Brain is just the weight of God –
For – Heft them – Pound for Pound –
And they will differ – if they do –
As Syllable from Sound.

Emily Dickinson (1830–1886), USA

259 Final reckoning

Nothing is at last sacred but the integrity of your own mind.

Ralph Waldo Emerson (1803–1882), USA

260 Thinking and being

Be a philosopher; but, amidst all your philosophy, be still a man.

David Hume (1711–1776), Scotland

261 Speech reveals

If you wish to know the mind
of a man, listen to his words.

Chinese proverb

262 On the contrary

Small minds are concerned
with the extraordinary,
great minds with the ordinary.

Blaise Pascal (1623–1662), France

263 On the couch

The science of the mind can only have
for its proper goal the understanding
of human nature by every human being,
and through its use, can bring peace to
every human soul.

Alfred Adler (1870–1937), Austria

264 Soul food

The cultivation of the mind is a kind
of food supplied for the soul of man.

Cicero (c.106–43 BCE), Rome

265 Back to the source

The conscious mind may be
compared to a fountain playing
in the sun and falling back into
the great subterranean pool of
unconscious from which it rises.

Sigmund Freud (1856–1939), Austria

266 Intuition

There comes a time when the
mind takes a higher plane of
knowledge but can never prove
how it got there.

*Anonymous (often mistakenly
attributed to Albert Einstein)*

267 Variations

Logicians have but ill defined
As rational the human mind.
Logic, they say, belongs to man,
But let them prove it if they can.

Oliver Goldsmith (1728–1774),
Ireland/England

Thought

268 Everything comes

You do not need to leave your room.
Remain sitting at your table and listen.
Do not even listen, simply wait.
Do not even wait, be quite still and solitary.
The world will freely offer itself to you
to be unmasked, it has no choice,
it will roll in ecstasy at your feet.

Franz Kafka (1883–1924), Austria

269 Murmurings

Thinking: The talking of the soul with itself.

Plato (c.429–c.347 BCE), Greece

270 Perfect timing

An invasion of armies can be resisted,
but not an idea whose time has come.

Victor Hugo (1802–1885), France

271 Windfalls

The thoughts that come often unsought, and, as it were, drop into the mind, are commonly the most valuable of any we have.

John Locke (1632–1704), England

272 Way back

The ancestor of every action
is a thought.

Ralph Waldo Emerson (1803–1882), USA

273 *The complete sailor*

Thought is the wind, knowledge the sail and mankind the vessel.

Augustus Hare (1792–1834), England

274 Dark reflections

Thoughts are the shadows of our feelings —
always darker, emptier and simpler.

Friedrich Nietzsche (1844–1900), Germany

275 Vital spark

Thought is only a flash between two long nights,
but this flash is everything.

Henri Poincaré (1854–1912), France

276 Creative thinking

We are what we think.
All that we are arises with our thoughts.
With our thoughts, we make the world.

The Buddha (c.563–c.483 BCE),
in the Dhammapada, *India*

277 Hammer and chisel

Thought is the sculptor who can create
the person you want to be.

Henry David Thoreau (1817–1862), USA

278 Mind

Mind in its purest play is like some bat
That beats about in caverns all alone,
Contriving by a kind of senseless wit
Not to conclude against a wall of stone.

It has no need to falter or explore;
Darkly it knows what obstacles are there,
And so may weave and flitter, dip and soar
In perfect courses through the blackest air.

And has this simile a like perfection?
The mind is like a bat. Precisely. Save
That in the very happiest intellection
A graceful error may correct the cave.

Richard Wilbur (b.1921), USA

279 Bored rebel

Men fear thought as they fear nothing else
on earth – more than ruin – more even
than death ... Thought is subversive and
revolutionary, destructive and terrible,
thought is merciless to privilege, established
institutions, and comfortable habit.

Bertrand Russell (1872–1970), England/USA

Happiness

280 Far and near

The foolish man seeks happiness in the distance;
the wise grows it under his feet.

James Oppenheim (1882–1932), USA

281 Cutting free

The essence of philosophy is that a man should so live that his happiness shall depend as little as possible on external things.

Epictetus (c.55 – c.135), Greece

282 Striding forth

I am more and more convinced that our happiness or our unhappiness depends far more on the way we meet the events of life than on the nature of those events themselves.

Karl Wilhelm von Humboldt (1767–1835), Germany

283 Simply put

There is only one happiness in life,
to love and be loved.

George Sand (1804–1876), France

284 Your decision

Most folks are about as happy as
they make up their minds to be.

Abraham Lincoln (1809–1865), USA

285 Modest total

I have diligently numbered the
days of pure and genuine happiness
which have fallen to my lot:
they amount to fourteen.

Abd-ar-Rahman III (912–961), Spain

286 A mystery

Happiness is a mystery like religion,
and it should never be rationalized.

G.K. Chesterton (1874–1936), England

287 Performance art

Happiness is an expression of the soul
in considered actions.

Aristotle (384–322 BCE), Greece

288 Pleasant thoughts

I have resolved from this day on,
I will do all the business I can honestly,
have all the fun I can reasonably,
do all the good I can willingly,
and save my digestion by thinking pleasantly.

Robert Louis Stevenson (1850 – 1894), Scotland

289 Coming close

To be kind to all, to like many and love a few,
to be needed and wanted by those we love,
is certainly the nearest we can come to happiness.

Mary, Queen of Scots (1542 – 1587), Scotland/England

290 On the wing

Happiness is like a butterfly which,
when pursued, is always beyond our grasp,
but, if you will sit down quietly,
may alight upon you.

Nathaniel Hawthorne (1804–1864), USA

291 Always no

Ask yourself whether you are happy and
you cease to be so.

John Stuart Mill (1806–1873), England

292 Green fingers

Let us be grateful to people
who make us happy, they are the
charming gardeners who make
our souls blossom.

Marcel Proust (1871–1922), France

293 Perfect balance

Happiness is when what you think,
what you say, and what you do are
in harmony.

Mahatma Gandhi (1869–1948), India

Personal growth

294 Destiny's path

Be fearless and pure; never waver in your determination
or your dedication to the spiritual life. Give freely. Be
self-controlled, sincere, truthful, loving, and full of the
desire to serve ... Learn to be detached and to take joy
in renunciation. Do not get angry or harm any living
creature, but be compassionate and gentle; show good
will to all. Cultivate vigour, patience, will, purity; avoid
malice and pride. Then, you will achieve your destiny.

Lord Krishna, in the Bhagavad Gita *(1st–2nd century* BCE*), India*

295 Letting go

The important thing is this: to be able at any
moment to sacrifice what we are for what we
could become.

Charles Edouard Dubois (1847–1885), USA/France

296 Work experience

As an irrigator guides water to his fields,
as an archer aims an arrow,
as a carpenter carves wood,
the wise shape their lives.

The Buddha (c.563–c.483 BCE), in the Dhammapada, *India*

297 Mirror image

Self-observation brings man to the realization of the
necessity of self-change. And in observing himself a
man notices that self-observation itself brings about
certain changes in his inner processes. He begins to
understand that self-observation is an instrument of
self-change, a means of awakening.

George Gurdjieff (1872–1949), Russia/France

298 Soul searching

Your vision will become clear only when you
can look into your own heart. Who looks
outside, dreams; who looks inside, awakens.

Carl Jung (1875–1961), Switzerland

299 *Higher dimensions*

The key to growth is the introduction
of higher dimensions of consciousness
into our awareness.

Lao Tzu (c.604–c.531 BCE), from the Tao Te Ching, *China*

300 *Never static*

All appears to change when
we change.

Henri Frédéric Amiel (1821–1881), Switzerland

301 Keeping focus

We must always change,
renew, rejuvenate ourselves;
otherwise, we harden.

Johann Wolfgang von Goethe (1749–1832), Germany

302 Blossom time

In a narrow circle the mind contracts.
Man grows with his expanded needs.

Friedrich von Schiller (1759–1805), Germany

303 Our calling

A musician must make music, an artist must paint,
a poet must write, if he is to be ultimately at peace
with himself. What a man can be, he must be.
This need we call self-actualization.

Abraham Maslow (1908–1970), USA

304 Transcendence

Nirvana is where there is no birth, no extinction.
It is seeing into the state of suchness, absolutely
transcending all the categories constructed by the
mind, for it is the Buddha's inner consciousness.

The Buddha (c.563 – c.483 BCE),
in the Lankavatara Sutra, *India*

305 Daybreak

Nirvana is not the blowing out of the candle. It is
the extinguishing of the flame because day is come.

Rabindranath Tagore (1861 – 1941), India

Faith

In times of darkness

Prayer

Loss and separation

Destiny

Hope

Security

Mortality

In times of darkness

306 Bittersweet

If we had no winter, the spring would not be so pleasant;
if we did not sometimes taste of adversity, prosperity
would not be so welcome.

Anne Bradstreet (c.1612–1672), England/USA

307 Trial by fire

Character cannot be developed in ease and quiet.
Only through experience of trial and suffering can
the soul be strengthened, vision cleared, ambition
inspired, and success achieved.

Attributed to Helen Keller (1880–1968), USA

308 Faith and redemption

The Lord redeemeth the soul of his servants:
and none of them that trust in him shall be desolate.

Psalms 34:22

309 Don't explain

To one who has faith, no explanation is necessary.
To one without faith, no explanation is possible.

Thomas Aquinas (1225–1274), Italy/France

310 Prayer to Great Spirit

Oh, Great Spirit,
whose voice I hear in the winds
and whose breath gives life to all the world, hear me.
I am small and weak.
I need your strength and wisdom.

Let me walk in beauty and make my eyes
ever behold the red and purple sunset.
Make my hands respect the things you have made
and my ears sharp to hear your voice.
Make me wise so that I may understand
the things you have taught my people.
Let me learn the lessons you have hidden
in every leaf and rock.

I seek strength, not to be superior to my brother,
but to fight my greatest enemy – myself.
Make me always ready to come to you
with clean hands and straight eyes,
so when life fades, as the fading sunset,
my spirit will come to you
without shame.

Chief Yellow Lark (19th/20th century), USA

Prayer

311 Beyond the self

Prayer is more than meditation.
In meditation the source of strength is
one's self. When one prays he goes to a
source of strength greater than his own.

*Madame Chiang Kai-shek (1897–2003),
China/USA*

312 Divine foresight

I have had prayers answered – most
strangely so sometimes – but I think
our heavenly Father's loving-kindness has
been even more evident in what He has
refused me.

Lewis Carroll (1832–1898), England

313 Praise the One

O God!
I go to sleep, awaken, live and die by You
and to You is the final gathering.
I go to sleep and the evening has come
with the Dominion belonging to the God.
All praise is due to God,
there is no partner with Him,
there is none worthy of worship besides Him,
and to Him is the final gathering.

Prophet Muhammad (c. 570–632), Saudi Arabia

314 In Orbit

May my prayers launch themselves
without drama and without damage,
trailing behind them all my years of striving.

May these purposeful parts of me
enter the orbit where they become me well,
glinting in space like a satellite
before a successful re-entry.

Jack Horniman (1940–1996), New Zealand

315 Kyrie

Because we cannot be clever and honest
And are inventors of things more intricate
Than the snowflake – Lord have mercy.

Because we are full of pride
In our humility, and because we believe
In our disbelief – Lord have mercy.

Because we will protect ourselves
From ourselves to the point
Of destroying ourselves – Lord have mercy.

And because on the slope to perfection,
When we should be half-way up,
We are half-way down – Lord have mercy.

R.S. Thomas (1913–2000), Wales

316 Prayer's teachings

No man ever prayed heartily without learning something.

Ralph Waldo Emerson (1803–1882), USA

317 Grateful thanks

You pray in your distress and in your need: would that you might pray also in the fullness of your joy and in your days of abundance.

Kahlil Gibran (1883–1931), Lebanon

318 Unseen effect

Prayer is an invisible tool which is wielded in a visible world.

Leo Tolstoy (1828–1910), Russia

319 Soul's transformation

Prayer is exhaling the spirit of man and inhaling the spirit of God.

Edwin Keith Thompson (1919–1960), USA

320 Reciprocity

Prayers go up and blessings
come down.

Yiddish proverb

Loss and separation

321 Gone to bed

Good-night! Good-night! as we so oft have said
Beneath this roof at midnight, in the days
That are no more, and shall no more return.
Thou hast but taken up thy lamp and gone to bed;
I stay a little longer, as one stays
To cover up the embers that still burn.

Henry Wadsworth Longfellow (1807–1882), USA

322 Consolation

While we are mourning the loss of our friend,
others are rejoicing to meet him behind the veil.

John Taylor (1753–1824), USA

323 Felix Randal

Felix Randal the farrier, O is he dead then? my duty all ended,
Who have watched his mould of man, bigboned and hardy-handsome
Pining, pining, till time when reason rambled in it, and some
Fatal four disorders, fleshed there, all contended?

Sickness broke him. Impatient, he cursed at first, but mended
Being anointed and all; tho' a heavenlier heart began some
Months earlier, since I had our sweet reprieve and ransom
Tendered to him. Ah well, God rest him all road ever he offended!

This seeing the sick endears them to us, us too it endears.
My tongue had taught thee comfort, touch had quenched thy tears,
Thy tears that touched my heart, child, Felix, poor Felix Randal;

How far from then forethought of, all thy more boisterous years,
When thou at the random grim forge, powerful amidst peers
Didst fettle for the great grey drayhorse his bright and
        battering sandal!

Gerard Manley Hopkins (1844–1889), England

324 Still around

People do not die for us immediately,
but remain bathed in a sort of aura of life
which bears no relation to true immortality
but through which they continue to occupy
our thoughts in the same way as when
they were alive. It is as though they were
travelling abroad.

Marcel Proust (1871–1922), France

325 Path to awakening

Man must be disappointed with the lesser
things of life before he can comprehend the
full value of the greater.

Edward Bulwer-Lytton (1803–1873), England

326 *Stormy weather*

Disappointments are to the soul
what the thunderstorm is to the air.

Friedrich von Schiller (1759–1805), Germany

327 Discoveries

The true power of love will often be unrecognized till the moment of parting is upon you.

Juliana Pereira (1895–1976), Portugal

328 Only natural

Loss is nothing else but change, and change is Nature's delight.

Marcus Aurelius (121–180), Rome

Destiny

329 Achieve your fate

Destiny is not a matter of chance: it is a matter of choice.
It is not something to be waited for; but, rather, something
to be achieved.

William Jennings Bryan (1860–1925), USA

330 Here for a reason

Your profession is not what brings home your paycheck.
Your profession is what you were put on earth to do.
With such passion and such intensity that it becomes
    spiritual in calling.

Vincent van Gogh (1853–1890), Netherlands/France

331 Intersection

Where your talents and the
needs of the world cross
lies your calling.

Aristotle (384–322 BCE), Greece

332 Broad view

Each man has his own vocation;
his talent is his call. There is one
direction in which all space is
open to him.

Ralph Waldo Emerson (1803–1882), USA

333 Needlework

Destiny itself is like a wonderful wide
tapestry in which every thread is guided
by an unspeakably tender hand, placed
beside another thread and held and
carried by a hundred others.

Rainer Maria Rilke (1875–1926), Austria/Germany

334 Special agenda

Destiny grants us our wishes, but in its
own way, in order to give us something
beyond our wishes.

*Johann Wolfgang von Goethe (1749–1832),
Germany*

335 The web of life

Humankind has not woven the web of life.
We are but one thread within it.
Whatever we do to the web,
    we do to ourselves.
All things are bound together.
All things connect.

Chief Seathl (1786–1866), USA

336 The Buddha's last words

All conditioned things are impermanent.
Work out your own salvation with diligence.

The Buddha (c.563–c.483 BCE), India

337 Doctor's encouragement

Your aspirations are your possibilities.

Samuel Johnson (1709–1784), England

338 Inescapable

A person often meets his destiny
on the road he took to avoid it.

Jean de La Fontaine (1621–1695), France

339 Ready or not

The willing, Destiny guides them;
the unwilling, Destiny drags them.

Seneca (c.4 BCE–c.65 CE), Rome

340 *Sampling the sea*

If a man wants to know the taste of sea water,
he only has to set off and go straight ahead.
If he keeps going, he is sure to come to the sea.
Dipping his finger into it and licking off the drops,
at that moment he knows for himself the taste
of all the seven oceans.

Hakuin (1685–1768), Japan

Hope

341 True passage

I steer my bark with hope in the head, leaving fear astern.
My hopes indeed sometimes fail, but not oftener than the
forebodings of the gloomy.

Thomas Jefferson (1743–1826), USA

342 Listen and see

In the night of death, hope sees a star,
and listening love can hear the rustle of a wing.

Robert Green Ingersoll (1833–1899), USA

343 Waiting patiently

To love, and bear; to hope till Hope creates
From its own wreck the thing it contemplates.

Percy Bysshe Shelley (1792–1822), England/Italy

344 Nature notes

If I keep a green bough in my heart,
then the singing bird will come.

Chinese proverb

345 Silent jig

He that liveth in hope danceth without music.

George Herbert (1593–1633), England

346 Bird of paradise

Hope is the thing with feathers
That perches in the soul –
And sings the tunes without the words –
And never stops at all.

Emily Dickinson (1830–1886), USA

347 Consequences

Each time a man stands up for
an ideal ... he sends forth a
tiny ripple of hope.

Robert Kennedy (1925–1968), USA

348 Double fault

At first we hope too much;
later on, not enough.

Joseph Roux (1725–1793), France

349 *All night long*

Hope is patience with the lamp lit.

Tertullian (c.155–230), North Africa

350 *Well provided*

He who has health
has hope; and he who
has hope has everything.

Arabian proverb

Security

351 Head above the sand

To keep oneself safe does not mean to bury oneself.

Seneca (c.4 BCE – c.65 CE), Rome

352 A daring adventure

Security is mostly a superstition.
It does not exist in nature,
nor do the children of men
as a whole experience it.
Avoiding danger is no safer in the
long run than outright exposure.
Life is either a daring adventure,
or nothing.

Attributed to Helen Keller (1880–1968), USA

353 Warning to a prince

A man may build himself a throne of bayonets,
but he cannot sit on it.

William Ralph Inge (1860–1954), England

354 Foolish bargain

Those who would give up Essential Liberty
to purchase a little Temporary Safety, deserve
neither Liberty nor Safety.

Benjamin Franklin (1706–1790), USA

355 Life force

Nothing is secure but life,
transition, the energizing spirit.

Ralph Waldo Emerson (1803–1882), USA

356 False friend

Security is mortals' chiefest enemy.

William Shakespeare (1564–1616), from Macbeth, *England*

Mortality

357 Goodbye to the soul

Vital spark of heav'nly flame!
Quit, oh quit, this mortal frame!
Trembling, hoping, ling'ring, flying,
Oh, the pain, the bliss of dying!
Hark! they whisper; angels say,
Sister Spirit, come away!

Alexander Pope (1688–1744), England

358 Celestial freedom

When the soul is in silent quietness it arises
    and leaves the body,
And reaching the Supreme Spirit finds there
    its body of light.
It is the land of infinite liberty where, beyond
    its mortal body, the Spirit of man is free.

From the Upanishads

359 On the other side

The soul is indestructible and its activity
will continue through eternity.
It is like the sun, which, to our eyes,
seems to set at night; but it has in reality
only gone to diffuse its light elsewhere.

Johann Wolfgang von Goethe (1749–1832),
Germany

360 Infinite morning

Today the journey is ended,
I have worked out the mandates of fate;
Naked, alone, undefended,
I knock at the Uttermost Gate.
Behind is life and its longing,
Its trial, its trouble, its sorrow,
Beyond is the Infinite Morning
Of a day without a tomorrow.

Wenonah Stevens Abbott (1865–1950), USA

361 White radiance

The splendours of the firmament of time
May be eclips'd, but are extinguish'd not;
Like stars to their appointed height they climb,
And death is a low mist which cannot blot
The brightness it may veil. When lofty thought
Lifts a young heart above its mortal lair,
And love and life contend in it for what
Shall be its earthly doom, the dead live there
And move like winds of light on dark and stormy air.

The One remains, the many change and pass;
Heaven's light forever shines, Earth's shadows fly;
Life, like a dome of many-coloured glass,
Stains the white radiance of Eternity.

Percy Bysshe Shelley (1792–1822), England/Italy

362 Dark Mother

Dark Mother, always gliding near, with soft feet,
Have none chanted for thee a chant of fullest welcome?

Then I chant it for thee – I glorify thee above all;
I bring thee a song that when thou must indeed come,
      come unfalteringly.

Approach, strong Deliveress!
When it is so – when thou hast taken them,
      I joyously sing the dead,
Lost in the loving, floating ocean of thee,
Laved in the flood of thy bliss, O Death.

From me to thee glad serenades,
Dances for thee I propose, saluting thee – adornments
      and feastings for thee;
And the sights of the open landscape, and the
      high-spread sky, are fitting,
And life and the fields, and the huge and thoughtful night.

The night, in silence, under many a star;
The ocean shore, and the husky whispering wave,
      whose voice I know;
And the soul turning to thee, O vast and well-veil'd
      Death,
And the body gratefully nestling close to thee.

Over the tree-tops I float thee a song!
Over the rising and sinking waves – over the myriad
      fields, and the prairies wide;
Over the dense-pack'd cities all, and the teeming
      wharves and ways,
I float this carol with joy, with joy to thee, O Death!

Walt Whitman (1819–1892), from Leaves of Grass, *USA*

363 Against the light

Her face is steadfast toward the shadowy land,
For dim beyond it looms the light of day;
Her feet are steadfast; all the arduous way
That foot-track hath not wavered on the sand.
She stands there like a beacon thro' the night,
A pale clear beacon where the storm-drift is;
She stands alone, a wonder deathly white;
She stands there patient, nerved with inner might,
Indomitable in her feebleness,
Her face and will athirst against the light.

Christina Georgina Rossetti (1830–1894), England

364 Time for change

There is no death.
Only a change of worlds.

Chief Seathl (1786–1866), USA

365 *Evanescence*

For what is it to die,
But to stand in the sun and melt
  into the wind?

Kahlil Gibran (1883–1931), Lebanon

Index of first lines

Index of authors and sources

Acknowledgments

Acknowledgments have been listed by quotation number.

1 from POLITICAL AND NATIONAL LIFE AND AFFAIRS by M.K. Gandhi, reprinted by permission of the Navajivan Trust (Estate of Mohandas K. Gandhi); **2** from MEMORIES, DREAMS AND REFLECTIONS by C.G. Jung, edited by Aniela Jaffe, translated by Richard & Clara Winston, copyright ©1961, 1962, 1963 and renewed 1989, 1990, 1991 by Random House, Inc. Used by permission of Pantheon Books, a division of Random House, Inc., and HarperCollins Ltd.; **4** from MOTHER NIGHT by Kurt Vonnegut (Harper & Row, 1966). Reprinted by permission of the Farber Literary Agency as the literary representative of the estate of Kurt Vonnegut; **5** from PHILOSOPHICAL INVESTIGATIONS by Ludwig Wittgenstein (Macmillan & Co Ltd, 1958). Reprinted by permission of the Master and Fellows, Trinity College, Cambridge; **6, 15, 197, 237, 241, 327** translations copyright © Duncan Baird Publishers, London 2007; **10** from ILLUSIONS: THE ADVENTURES OF A RELUCTANT MESSIAH by Richard Bach (Dell, 1989). Reprinted by permission of Random House, Inc. US; **17** from FOUR ARCHETYPES by Carl Jung (Routledge and K. Paul, 1972). Reproduced by permission of Taylor & Francis books UK, and Preston University Press; **41, 148** from Longchenpa: KINDLY BENT TO EASE US – PART ONE: MIND, translated and annotated by Herbert V. Guenther (Dharma Publishing, 1975). Reprinted by permission of Dharma Publishing;

49 from "To The Sun" from THE COLLECTED POEMS OF KATHLEEN RAINE, Golgonooza Press, Ipswitch, 2000. Copyright © Kathleen Raine 2000. Reprinted by permission of Golgonooza (UK) and Counterpoint Press (US), a member of Perseus Books Group;

68 from THE LIFE OF DYLAN THOMAS by Constantine Fitzgibbon (J.M. Dent & Sons, 1966). Reprinted by permission of David Higham Associates, London;

70 attributed to Edmund Morrison, precise source unknown. Reprinted by permission of Wordsworth Editions Ltd.;

77 from THE DIONYSIAN SELF: C.G. JUNG'S RECEPTION OF FRIEDRICH NIETZSCHE by Paul Bishop (Walter de Gruyter, 1995). Reprinted by permission of the publishers;

80 from THE DIVINE MILIEU by Pierre Teilhard de Chardin © 1957 by Editions du Seuil, Paris. English translation © 1960 by Wm. Collins Sons & Co., London, and Harper & Row Publishers, Inc., New York. Renewed © 1988 by Harper & Row Publishers, Inc. Reprinted by permission of HarperCollins Publishers and HarperCollins Ltd.;

82 from THE INDIVIDUAL PSYCHOLOGY OF ALFRED ADLER by H. Ansbacher & R. Ansbacher (Harper Perennial, 1964). Reprinted by permission of David Higham Associates, London;

89 from SURPRISED BY JOY: THE SHAPE OF MY EARLY LIFE by C.S. Lewis (Harvest Books, 1966). Copyright © C.S. Lewis Pte. Ltd.;

105 from BACK TO METHUSELAH by George Bernard Shaw (Constable, 1928). Reprinted by permission of The Society of Authors, on behalf of the Estate of Bernard Shaw;

118 from THE SCREWTAPE LETTERS by C.S. Lewis (MacMillan, 1946). Copyright © C.S. Lewis Pte. Ltd.;

119 from a speech by Winston Churchill. Reproduced with permission of Curtis Brown Ltd., London, on behalf of The Estate of Winston Churchill. Copyright © Winston S. Churchill;

125, 293 attributed to M.K. Gandhi, precise source unknown. Reprinted by permission of the Navajivan Trust (Estate of Mohandas K. Gandhi);

136 from THE FOUR-CHAMBERED HEART by Anaïs Nin (Swallow Press, 1959). Copyright © 1959, 1974 by Anaïs Nin. All rights reserved. Reprinted by permission of the Author's Representative, Barbara W. Stuhlmann, and the publishers;

139 from THE AUTOBIOGRAPHY OF BERTRAND RUSSELL by Bertrand Russell (Routledge, 2000). Reproduced by permission of Taylor & Francis Books UK, and The Bertrand Russell Peace Foundation Ltd.;

144 reprinted by permission of The Office of His Holiness the Dalai Lama;

154 from TRANSFORMATION & HEALING: SUTRA ON THE FOUR ESTABLISHMENTS OF MINDFULNESS (1990, 2006) by Thich Nhat Hanh with permission of Parallax Press, Berkeley, California, www.parallax.org;

171 from THE DIARY OF A YOUNG GIRL: THE DEFINITIVE EDITION by Anne Frank, edited by Otto H. Frank and Mirjam Pressler, translated by Susan Massotty (Viking 1997), copyright © The Anne Frank-Fonds, Basle, Switzerland, 1991. English translation copyright © Doubleday, a division of Bantam Doubleday Dell Publishing Group, Inc., 1995. Reproduced by permission of Penguin Books Ltd., and Doubleday, a division of Random House, Inc.;

198 from J.M. Barrie's PETER PAN reproduced with kind permission of Great Ormond Street Hospital for Children, London;

200 from a letter to P. Moos, March 30, 1950 by Albert Einstein. Reprinted with permission of The Albert Einstein Archives of the Hebrew University of Jerusalem;

203 attributed to Anaïs Nin, precise source unknown. Copyright © The Anaïs Nin Trust. All rights reserved. Reprinted by permission of the Author's

Representative, Barbara W. Stuhlmann;
209 from THE LIFE OF REASON by
George Santayana (Prometheus Books,
1998). Reprinted by permission of
the publishers;
216 attributed to Reinhold Niebuhr,
precise source unknown. Reprinted by
permission of The Haworth Press, Inc.;
243 attributed to C.S. Lewis, precise
source unknown. Copyright © C.S.
Lewis Pte. Ltd.;
258 from THE POEMS OF EMILY
DICKINSON: READING EDITION
edited by Ralph W. Franklin, F598,
Cambridge, Mass.: The Belknap Press of
Harvard University Press, Copyright ©
1998, 1999 by the President and Fellows
of Harvard College. Copyright © 1951,
1955, 1979, 1983 by the President and
Fellows of Harvard College. Reprinted
by permission of the publishers, and the
Trustees of Amherst College;
278 "Mind" in THINGS OF THIS WORLD,
copyright ©1956 and renewed 1984 by
Richard Wilbur, reprinted by permission

of Harcourt, Inc., and from COLLECTED
POEMS by Richard Wilbur (Harvest
Books, 2006). Reprinted by permission of
Faber and Faber Ltd.;
279 from WHY MEN FIGHT by
Bertrand Russell (The Century Company,
1917). Reprinted by permission of The
Bertrand Russell Peace Foundation Ltd.;
303 from MASLOW ON
MANAGEMENT by Abraham H.
Maslow (John Wiley & Sons, Inc.,
1998). Reprinted by permission of
the publishers;
305 attributed to Rabindranath Tagore,
precise source unknown. Reprinted by
permission of Visva-Bharati University;
314 copyright © DBP;
315 from COLLECTED LATER POEMS
by R.S. Thomas (Bloodaxe Books,
2004). Reprinted by permission of
the publishers;
333 from LETTERS TO A YOUNG
POET by Rainer Maria Rilke. Copyright
© 2000 by Rainer Maria Rilke. Reprinted
with permission of New World Library,

Novato, CA. www.newworldlibrary.com;
346 from THE POEMS OF EMILY
DICKINSON: READING EDITION
edited by Ralph W. Franklin, F598,
Cambridge, Mass.: The Belknap Press of
Harvard University Press, Copyright ©
1998, 1999 by the President and Fellows
of Harvard College. Copyright © 1951,
1955, 1979, 1983 by the President and
Fellows of Harvard College. Reprinted
by permission of the publishers, and
the Trustees of Amherst College;
353 from THE WIT AND WISDOM
OF DEAN INGE by William Ralph
Inge (Longmans, Green & Co., 1927).
Reprinted by permission of Mr Chris
Inge of Churton Inge Associates
(The Estate of Dean Inge);
365 from THE PROPHET by Kahlil
Gibran, copyright 1923 by Kahlil Gibran
and renewed 1951 by Administrators
C.T.A. of Kahlil Gibran Estate and Mary G.
Gibran. Used by permission of Alfred A.
Knopf, a division of Random House, Inc.

The publishers have made every effort
to trace copyright holders, but if anyone
has been omitted we apologize and
will, if informed, make corrections in
any future edition.

Photographic credits

The publisher would like to thank the following people and photographic libraries for permission to reproduce their material. Every care has been taken to trace copyright holders. However, if we have omitted anyone we apologize and will, if informed, make corrections in future printings.

Page: 2 Anne Laird/Corbis; **5** Gary W. Carter/Corbis; **6-7** Pat O'Hara/Getty; **8-9** Pete Leonard/Corbis; **11** A. Green/Corbis; **13** Pete Leonard/Corbis; **14-15** Johner/Getty; **16** Art Wolfe/Getty; **20** Kennan Ward/Corbis; **24** Klaus Hackenberg/Corbis; **26-27** Darlyne A. Murawski/Getty; **29** Art Wolfe/Getty; **30-31** Andy Rouse/NHPA; **34-35** Jeff Hunter/Getty; **38-39** Jim Erickson/Corbis; **40-41** Marianne Majerus; **43** Lee White/Corbis; **45** Bob Elsdale/Getty; **46-47** Tom Falks/Getty; **49** Rob Howard/Corbis; **52-53** B.S.P.I./Corbis; **57** Nightlight/Corbis; **58-59** Duncan Maxwell/Corbis; **62-63** Marianne Majerus; **64-65** Steve Satushek/Getty; **68-69** Paul Cherfils/Getty; **72-73** Marianne Majerus; **74-75** Briggitte Sporrer/Corbis; **78-79** DAJ/Getty; **81** Gordon Osmundson/Corbis; **82-83** Jim Zuckerman/Corbis; **86-87** Roman Soumar/Corbis; **96-97** Ron Watts/Corbis; **100-101** Rob & SAS/Corbis; **102-103** Peter Dyballa/Corbis; **107** John Shaw/NHPA; **110-111** Massimo Listri/Corbis; **116-117** Bohemian Nomad Picturemaker/Corbis; **118-119** Tom Bean/Corbis; **120-121** Darrell Gulin/Corbis; **124-125** Scott Cunningham/Getty; **129** Darrell Gulin/Corbis; **132** Grant. V. Faint/Getty; **134** Marianne Majerus; **137** Nathan Bilow/Getty; **140-141** Ed Clark/Getty; **144-145** Michael Melford/Getty; **146-147** Peter Adam/Corbis; **150** Guntmar Fritz/Corbis; **152** Doug Plummer/Getty; **157** Frithjof Hirdes/